THE EARLY YEARS INSPECTION PROGRAMME Workbook

CONGRATULATIONS

on purchasing The Early Years Inspection Programme.

Setting yourself a goal to work towards being confident when you have your Early Years Inspection is paramount.

The purpose of this book is so you can keep everything in one place and have it to hand when you need it.

Take each module one step at a time.
Be prepared to SHINE and showcase
how you are adding IMPACT in your setting.

Love the Jigsaw Team

MODULE ONE:
Lesson One

QUALITY IMPROVEMENT

Checklist

Audit toolkit linking to
Education Inspection Framework

2021/2022

SETTING
Details

Name of setting:

Date of last inspection or registration:

Grade:

Using the recommendations from your last inspection - write how you have improved.
These will be your Lines of Enquiry (LOE) or Area of Focus (AOF) for your next inspection:

LOE 1.

LOE 2.

LOE 3.

LOE 4.

SETTING
Details

Manager's name:

Qualifications:

Deputy Manager's name:

SENCO:

Designated Safeguarding Lead:

Children on roll:

EAL Children:

SEN Children:

Qualifications of staff:

Level 6:

Number of agency staff:

Level 5:

Level 4:

Confirm all agency staff know safeguarding procedures: ✓

Level 3:

Level 2:

Confirm all staff's First Aid qualifications are up to date: ✓

Unqualified:

ANY
other details

Look at the statements and circle which RAG rating you are currently at.
Green for good, **Amber** for needs some improving, **Red** for needs changing now.

If you are in the Amber and Red section, write what you need to do to improve.

1. Ofsted Registration Certificate: ● ● ●

> Any actions?

2. Public Liability Insurance Certificate: ● ● ●

> Any actions?

3. Complaints poster and number: ● ● ●

> Any actions?

4. Mobile phones - storing and policy: ● ● ●

> Any actions?

5. Policies and procedures - last updated etc.   ● ● ●

> Any actions?

6. Check staff training certificates: ● ● ●

> Any actions?

7. Check all children's attendance records in relation to date and time: ● ● ●

> Any actions?

8. Check medicines and accident records: ● ● ●

> Any actions?

Look at the statements and circle which RAG rating you are currently at.
Green for good, **Amber** for needs some improving, **Red** for needs changing now.

If you are in the Amber and Red section, write what you need to do to improve.

9. Check evaluations for the practice - when was this last done? ● ● ●

Any actions?

10. Check visitors policy and procedures: ● ● ●

Any actions?

11. Check last drill and evacuation and policy date: ● ● ●

Any actions?

12. Check all First Aid qualifications are up to date: ● ● ●

Any actions?

13. Check how you evidence partnerships with parents - even through lockdown: ● ● ●

Any actions?

14. Check how you work in partnership with outside agencies: ● ● ●

Any actions?

15. Check how well staff are gaining more knowledge and improving their skills: ● ● ●

Any actions?

16. Check the last training course attended. What was the impact? ● ● ●

Any actions?

Look at the statements and circle which RAG rating you are currently at.
Green for good, **Amber** for needs some improving, **Red** for needs changing now.

If you are in the Amber and Red section, write what you need to do to improve.

17. Check supervisions and appraisals are up to date: ● ● ●

Any actions?

18. Check staff know their targets from their last supervision: ● ● ●

Any actions?

19. Check your induction process. Have these all been completed? ● ● ●

Any actions?

20. Check all staff have two satisfactory references: ● ● ●

Any actions?

21. Check how well you are supporting the well-being of staff: ● ● ●

Any actions?

22. Check how well you are being supported for your own well-being: ● ● ●

Any actions?

23. Check all staff are up to date with Safeguarding training: ● ● ●

Any actions?

24. Check all staff understand Prevent Duty and FGM: ● ● ●

Any actions?

Look at the statements and circle which RAG rating you are currently at.
Green for good, **Amber** for needs some improving, **Red** for needs changing now.

If you are in the Amber and Red section, write what you need to do to improve.

25. Check all staff understand County Lines?   ● ● ●

Any actions?

26. Check staff are all aware of who to go to if they have concerns about another staff member: ● ● ●

Any actions?

27. Check staff understand the activities that can support British Values: ● ● ●

Any actions?

28. Check staff understand how the experiences they provide support children's Cultural Capital: ● ● ●

Any actions?

29. Check your own supervision and appraisals. When were they completed?   ● ● ●

Any actions?

30. Check how you evaluate your setting: ● ● ●

Any actions?

What are the settings strengths?

Any actions?

What areas need to be improved in the setting?

Any actions?

QUALITY
of Education

Visit each room and record the following:

Name of room:

What is the intention of the day and why?

Which children are being focused on?

Why are you working on this intention?

Was it from a past observation?

How are you going to implement this?

Any actions or training which need to be addressed?

QUALITY
of Education

Visit each room and record the following:

Name of room:

What is the intention of the day and why?

Which children are being focused on?

Why are you working on this intention?

Was it from a past observation?

How are you going to implement this?

Any actions or training which need to be addressed?

QUALITY
of Education

Visit each room and record the following:

Name of room:

What is the intention of the day and why?

Which children are being focused on?

Why are you working on this intention?

Was it from a past observation?

How are you going to implement this?

Any actions or training which need to be addressed?

QUALITY
of Education

Visit each room and record the following:

Name of room:

What is the intention of the day and why?

Which children are being focused on?

Why are you working on this intention?

Was it from a past observation?

How are you going to implement this?

Any actions or training which need to be addressed?

QUALITY
of Education

Visit each room and record the following:

Name of room:

What is the intention of the day and why?

Which children are being focused on?

Why are you working on this intention?

Was it from a past observation?

How are you going to implement this?

Any actions or training which need to be addressed?

Look at the statements and circle which RAG rating you are currently at.
Green for good, **Amber** for needs some improving, **Red** for needs changing now.

If you are in the Amber and Red section, write what you need to do to improve.

31. Are all activities safe to use?

Any actions?

32. Are they age and stage appropriate?

Any actions?

33. Are all resources clean?

Any actions?

34. Are all children accessing all activities or are some left untouched?

Any actions?

35. Are the toilets replenished with soap, toilet paper and hand towels?

Any actions?

36. Has the indoor environment been risk assessed?

Any actions?

37. Has the outdoor environment been risk assessed?

Any actions?

38. Are all children engaged in play? No invisible children?

Any actions?

Look at the statements and circle which RAG rating you are currently at.
Green for good, **Amber** for needs some improving, **Red** for needs changing now.

If you are in the Amber and Red section, write what you need to do to improve.

39. Is the children's work displayed with purpose?

Any actions?

40. Check children's self-esteem is being promoted:

Any actions?

41. Check all staff know the setting's vision:

Any actions?

42. Check all staff are interacting with children at their level:

Any actions?

43. Check all staff are communicating with each other professionally:

Any actions?

BEHAVIOUR
and Attitudes

Look at the statements and circle which RAG rating you are currently at.
Green for good, **Amber** for needs some improving, **Red** for needs changing now.

If you are in the Amber and Red section, write what you need to do to improve.

44. Check children's emotional needs are met: ● ● ●

Any actions?

45. Check how behaviour is being monitored and managed: ● ● ●

Any actions?

46. Check how children are regulating their own behaviour: ● ● ●

Any actions?

47. Check how children are listening and understanding instructions: ● ● ●

Any actions?

48. Check how children are taking turns and sharing. Is this being promoted? ● ● ●

Any actions?

PERSONAL
Development

Look at the statements and circle which RAG rating you are currently at.
Green for good, **Amber** for needs some improving, **Red** for needs changing now.

If you are in the Amber and Red section, write what you need to do to improve.

49. Check children are given a rich set of experiences that promote their understanding of families and communities: ● ● ●

Any actions?

50. Check practitioners talk to children about their feelings: ● ● ●

Any actions?

51. Check children are able to take risks indoors and outdoors: ● ● ●

Any actions?

52. Check staff talk to children about keeping healthy - including oral health: ● ● ●

Any actions?

53. Check children are able to manage their personal needs effectively: ● ● ●

Any actions?

54. Check staff are supporting children to be confident, resilient and independent: ● ● ●

Any actions?

ACTION
Plan

MODULE ONE:
Lesson Two

Plan

MODULE ONE:
Lesson Three

SELF-EVALUATION
Toolkit

- Use the self evaluation toolkit within your setting to see where you honestly think you are on your journey.

- Tick the box at the side of the statement which represents you best.

- You will need to be totally honest with yourself and be prepared to make the changes to improve.

- Once you have this completed, talk to the rest of your team to see how you need to further improve.

- Use the target plan after each section to add your responses.

- Ensure those targets are SMART.

- Put a date in your diary to check these have been achieved.

LEADERSHIP
and Management

LEADERSHIP
and Management
OUTSTANDING

- Leaders ensure that they and practitioners receive focused and highly effective professional development. Practitioners' subject, pedagogical content and knowledge consistently builds and develops over time, and this translates into improvements in the teaching of the curriculum.

- Leaders ensure that highly effective and meaningful engagement takes place with staff at all levels and that any issues are identified. When issues are identified, in particular about workload, they are consistently dealt with appropriately and quickly.

- Staff routinely report high levels of support for well-being issues.

GOOD

In order for the effectiveness of leadership and management to be judged good, it must meet all of the following criteria:

- Leaders have a clear and ambitious vision for providing high-quality, inclusive care and education to all. This is realised through strong shared values, policies and practice.

- Leaders focus on improving practitioners' knowledge of the areas of learning and understanding of how children learn to enhance the teaching of the curriculum and appropriate use of assessment. The practice and subject knowledge of practitioners build and improve over time.

- Leaders have effective systems in place for the supervision and support of staff.

- Leaders act with integrity to ensure that all children, particularly those with SEND, have full access to their entitlement to early education.

- Leaders engage effectively with children, their parents and others in their community, including schools and other local services.

LEADERSHIP
and Management

GOOD

- Leaders engage with their staff and are aware of the main pressures on them. They are realistic and constructive in the way they manage staff, including their workload.

- Those with oversight or governance understand their role and carry this out effectively. They have a clear vision and strategy and hold senior leaders to account for the quality of care and education. They ensure that resources are managed sustainably, effectively and efficiently.

- The provider fulfils its statutory duties, for example under the Equality Act 2010, and other duties, for example in relation to the 'Prevent' strategy and safeguarding.

- Leaders protect staff from harassment, bullying and discrimination.

- The provider has a culture of safeguarding that facilitates effective arrangements to: identify children who may need early help or are at risk of neglect, abuse, grooming or exploitation; help children to reduce their risk of harm by securing the support they need, or referring in a timely way to those who have the expertise to help; and manage safe recruitment and allegations about adults who may be a risk to children.

REQUIRES IMPROVEMENT

- Leadership and management are not yet good.

- Any breaches of statutory requirements do not have a significant impact on children's safety, well-being or learning and development.

LEADERSHIP
and Management

INADEQUATE

Leadership and management are likely to be inadequate if one or more of the following applies:

- Leaders do not have the capacity to improve the quality of education and care. Actions taken to tackle areas of identified weakness have been insufficient or ineffective. Training for staff is ineffective.

- Leaders are not doing enough to tackle the poor curriculum or teaching, or the inappropriate use of assessment. This has a significant impact on children's progress, particularly those who are disadvantaged and those with SEND.

- Links with parents, other settings and professionals involved in supporting children's care and education do not identify or meet children's individual needs. Children fail to thrive.

- Leaders do not tackle instances of discrimination. Equality, Diversity and British Values are not actively promoted in practice.

- Safeguarding and welfare requirements are not met. Breaches have a significant impact on the safety and well-being of children.

TARGET
Action Plan

What do we need to do to improve on our Leadership and Management?

What is your INTENT?

1.
2.
3.
4.

How are we going to implement the INTENT?

1.
2.
3.
4.

What is the time frame to achieve your INTENT and who is responsible for this?

1.
2.
3.
4.

QUALITY
of Education

QUALITY
of Education

OUTSTANDING

The provider meets all the criteria for a good quality of education securely and consistently. The quality of education at this setting is exceptional. In addition, the following apply:

- The provider's curriculum intent and implementation are embedded securely and consistently across the provision. It is evident from what practitioners do that they have a firm and common understanding of the provider's curriculum intent and what it means for their practice. Across all parts of the provision, practitioners' interactions with children are of a high quality and contribute well to delivering the curriculum intent.

- Children's experiences over time are consistently and coherently arranged to build cumulatively sufficient knowledge and skills for their future learning.

- The impact of the curriculum on what children know, can remember and do is highly effective. Children demonstrate this through being deeply engaged in their work and play and sustaining high levels of concentration. Children, including those children from disadvantaged backgrounds, do well. Children with SEND achieve the best possible outcomes.

- Children consistently use new vocabulary that enables them to communicate effectively. They speak with increasing confidence and fluency, which means that they secure strong foundations for future learning, especially in preparation for them to become fluent readers.

QUALITY
of Education

GOOD

Intent

- Leaders adopt or construct a curriculum that is ambitious and designed to give children, particularly the most disadvantaged, the knowledge and Cultural Capital they need to succeed in life.

- The provider's curriculum is coherently planned and sequenced. It builds on what children know and can do, towards cumulatively sufficient knowledge and skills for their future learning.

- The provider has the same ambitions for almost all children. For children with particular needs, such as those with high levels of SEND, their curriculum is still ambitious and meets their needs.

Implementation

- Children benefit from meaningful learning across the EYFS curriculum.

- Practitioners understand the areas of learning they teach and the way in which young children learn. Leaders provide effective support for staff with less experience and knowledge of teaching.

- Practitioners present information clearly to children, promoting appropriate discussion about the subject matter being taught. They communicate well to check children's understanding, identify misconceptions and provide clear explanations to improve their learning. In so doing, they respond and adapt their teaching as necessary.

- Practitioners ensure that their own speaking, listening and reading of English enables children to hear and develop their own language and vocabulary well. They read to children in a way that excites and engages them, introducing new ideas, concepts and vocabulary.

QUALITY
of Education

GOOD
Implementation

- Over the EYFS, teaching is designed to help children remember long-term what they have been taught and to integrate new knowledge into larger concepts.

- Practitioners and leaders use assessment well to check what children know and can do to inform teaching. This includes planning suitably challenging activities and responding to specific needs. Leaders understand the limitations of assessment and avoid unnecessary burdens for staff or children.

- Practitioners and leaders create an environment that supports the intent of an ambitious and coherently planned and sequenced curriculum. The available resources meet the children's needs and promote their focus on learning.

- Practitioners share information with parents about their child's progress in relation to the EYFS. They help parents to support and extend their child's learning at home, including how to encourage a love of reading.

Impact

- Children develop detailed knowledge and skills across the seven areas of learning and use these in an age-appropriate way. Children develop their vocabulary and understanding of language across the EYFS curriculum.

- Children are ready for the next stage of education, especially school, where applicable. They have the knowledge and skills they need to benefit from what school has to offer when it is time to move on.

- Children enjoy, listen attentively and respond with comprehension to familiar stories, rhymes and songs that are appropriate to their age and stage of development.

QUALITY
of Education

GOOD
Impact

- Children understand securely the early mathematical concepts appropriate to their age and stage that will enable them to move on to the next stage of learning.

- Children articulate what they know, understand and can do in an age-appropriate way, holding thoughtful conversations with adults and their friends.

- From birth onwards, children are physically active in their play, developing their physiological, cardiovascular and motor skills. They show good control and coordination in both large and small movements appropriate for their stage of development.

REQUIRES IMPROVEMENT

- Provision is not good.

- Any breaches of the statutory requirements do not have a significant impact on children's learning and development.

QUALITY
of Education

INADEQUATE

The quality of education is likely to be inadequate
if one or more of the following applies:

- A poorly designed and implemented curriculum does not meet children's needs. The needs of babies and young children are not met.

- Practitioners have a poor understanding of the areas of learning they teach and the way in which young children learn.

- Assessment is overly burdensome. It is unhelpful in determining what children know, understand and can do.

- Children are not well prepared for school or the next stage of their learning, particularly those who are in receipt of additional funding. Strategies for engaging parents are weak and parents do not know what their child is learning or how they can help them improve.

- Breaches of the statutory requirements have a significant impact on children's learning and development.

TARGET
Action Plan

What do we need to do to improve on our Quality of Education?

What is your INTENT?

1.

2.

3.

4.

How are we going to implement the INTENT?

1.

2.

3.

4.

What is the time frame to achieve your INTENT and who is responsible for this?

1.

2.

3.

4.

BEHAVIOURS
and Attitudes

BEHAVIOURS
and Attitudes

OUTSTANDING

In order for behaviour and attitudes to be judged outstanding, they must meet all of the good criteria securely and consistently. They must also meet all the outstanding criteria:

- Children have consistently high levels of respect for others. They increasingly show high levels of confidence in social situations. They confidently demonstrate their understanding of why behaviour rules are in place and recognise the impact that their behaviour has on others.

- Children are highly motivated and are very eager to join in, share and co-operate with each other. They have consistently positive attitudes towards their play and learning.

- Children demonstrate high levels of self-control and consistently keep on trying hard, even if they encounter difficulties. When children struggle with this, leaders and practitioners take intelligent, swift and highly effective action to support them.

GOOD

- The provider has high expectations for children's behaviour and conduct. These expectations are commonly understood and applied consistently and fairly. This is reflected in children's positive behaviour and conduct. They are beginning to manage their own feelings and behaviour and to understand how these have an impact on others.

- When children struggle with regulating their behaviour, leaders and practitioners take appropriate action to support them. Children are developing a sense of right and wrong. Children demonstrate their positive attitudes to learning through high levels of curiosity, concentration and enjoyment. They listen intently and respond positively to adults and each other. Children are developing their resilience to setbacks and take pride in their achievements.

BEHAVIOURS
and Attitudes

GOOD

- Children benefit fully from the early education opportunities available to them by participating and responding promptly to requests and instructions from practitioners.

- Relationships among children, parents and staff reflect a positive and respectful culture. Children feel safe and secure.

REQUIRES IMPROVEMENT

- Children's behaviour and attitudes are not good.

- Any breaches of the statutory requirements do not have a significant impact on children's behaviour and attitudes.

INADEQUATE
Children's behaviour and attitudes are likely to be inadequate if one or both of the following apply:

- Children's behaviour and attitudes to learning are poor. Their frequent lack of engagement in activities and/or poor behaviour lead to a disorderly environment that hinders children's learning and/or puts themselves and others at risk.

- Children persistently demonstrate poor self-control and a lack of respect for others, leading to children not feeling safe and secure.

TARGET
Action Plan

What do we need to do to improve on our Behaviour and Attitudes?

What is your INTENT?

1.

2.

3.

4.

How are we going to implement the INTENT?

1.

2.

3.

4.

What is the time frame to achieve your INTENT and who is responsible for this?

1.

2.

3.

4.

PERSONAL
Development

PERSONAL
Development

OUTSTANDING

The provider meets all the criteria for good personal development securely and consistently. Personal development in this provision is exceptional. In addition, the following apply:

- The provider is highly successful at giving children a rich set of experiences that promote an understanding of people, families and communities beyond their own.

- Practitioners teach children the language of feelings, helping them to appropriately develop their emotional literacy.

- Practitioners value and understand the practice and principles of equality and diversity. They are effective at promoting these in an age-appropriate way, which includes routinely challenging stereotypical behaviours and respecting differences. This helps children to reflect on their differences and understand what makes them unique.

GOOD

- The curriculum and the provider's effective care practices promote and support children's emotional security and development of their character. Children are gaining a good understanding of what makes them unique.

- The curriculum and the provider's effective care practices promote children's confidence, resilience and independence. Practitioners teach children to take appropriate risks and challenges as they play and learn both inside and outdoors, particularly supporting them to develop physical and emotional health.

- A well-established key person system helps children form secure attachments and promotes their well-being and independence. Relationships between staff and babies are sensitive, stimulating and responsive.

PERSONAL
Development

GOOD

- Practitioners provide a healthy diet and a range of opportunities for physically active play, both inside and outdoors. They give clear and consistent messages to children that support healthy choices around food, rest, exercise and screen time.

- Practitioners help children to gain an effective understanding of when they might be at risk, including when using the internet, digital technology and social media and where to get support if they need it.

- Practitioners ensure that policies are implemented consistently. Hygiene practices ensure that the personal needs of children of all ages are met appropriately. Practitioners teach children to become increasingly independent in managing their personal needs.

- The provider prepares children for life in modern Britain by: equipping them to be respectful and to recognise those who help us and contribute positively to society; developing their understanding of fundamental British values; developing their understanding and appreciation of diversity; celebrating what we have in common and promoting respect for different people.

REQUIRES IMPROVEMENT

- Provision to support children's personal development is not good.

- Any breaches of the statutory requirements for safeguarding and welfare and/or learning and development do not have a significant impact on children's safety, well-being and personal development.

PERSONAL
Development

INADEQUATE

Personal development is likely to be inadequate if one or more of the following applies:

- Breaches of the statutory requirements have a significant impact on children's safety, well-being and personal development. Breaches of the statutory requirements have a significant impact on children's safety, well-being and personal development.

- Practitioners do not support children's social and emotional well-being or prepare them for transitions within the setting and/or to other settings and school.

- The key person system does not work effectively to support children's emotional well-being and children fail to form secure attachments with their carers. Babies are not stimulated.

- Policies, procedures and practice do not promote the health and welfare of children. As a result, children do not know how to keep themselves safe and healthy.

- Children have a narrow experience that does not promote their understanding of people and communities beyond their own or help them to recognise and accept each other's differences.

TARGET
Action Plan

What do we need to do to improve on our Personal Development?

What is your INTENT?

1.

2.

3.

4.

How are we going to implement the INTENT?

1.

2.

3.

4.

What is the time frame to achieve your INTENT and who is responsible for this?

1.

2.

3.

4.

MODULE ONE:
Lesson Four

LEADERSHIP
and Management

OUTSTANDING

- Leaders ensure that they and practitioners receive focused and highly effective professional development. Practitioners' subject, pedagogical content and knowledge consistently builds and develops over time, and this consistently translates into improvements in the teaching of the curriculum.

- Leaders ensure that highly effective and meaningful engagement takes place with staff at all levels and that any issues are identified. When issues are identified – in particular about workload – they are consistently dealt with appropriately and quickly.

- Staff consistently report high levels of support for well-being issues.

GOOD

In order for the effectiveness of leadership and management to be judged good, it must meet all of the following criteria:

- Leaders have a clear and ambitious vision for providing high-quality, inclusive care and education to all. This is realised through strong shared values, policies and practice.

- Leaders focus on improving practitioners' knowledge of the areas of learning and understanding of how children learn to enhance the teaching of the curriculum and appropriate use of assessment. The practice and subject knowledge of practitioners builds and improves over time. Leaders have effective systems in place for the supervision and support of staff.

- Leaders act with integrity to ensure that all children, particularly those with SEND, have full access to their entitlement to early education.

- Leaders engage effectively with children, their parents and others in their community, including schools and other local services.

LEADERSHIP
and Management

GOOD

- Leaders engage with their staff and are aware of the main pressures on them. They are realistic and constructive in the way they manage staff, including their workload.

- Those with oversight or governance understand their role and carry this out effectively. They have a clear vision and strategy and hold senior leaders to account for the quality of care and education. They ensure that resources are managed sustainably, effectively and efficiently.

- The provider fulfils its statutory duties, for example under the Equality Act 2010, and other duties, for example in relation to the 'Prevent' strategy and safeguarding.

- Leaders protect staff from harassment, bullying and discrimination.

- The provider has a culture of safeguarding that facilitates effective arrangements to: identify children who may need early help or are at risk of neglect, abuse, grooming or exploitation; help children to reduce their risk of harm by securing the support they need, or referring in a timely way to those who have the expertise to help; and manage safe recruitment and allegations about adults who may be a risk to children.

REQUIRES IMPROVEMENT

- Leadership and management are not yet good.

- Any breaches of statutory requirements do not have a significant impact on children's safety, well-being or learning and development.

LEADERSHIP
and Management
INADEQUATE

- Leadership and management are likely to be inadequate if one or more of the following applies.

- Leaders do not have the capacity to improve the quality of education and care. Actions taken to tackle areas of identified weakness have been insufficient or ineffective. Training for staff is ineffective.

- Leaders are not doing enough to tackle the poor curriculum or teaching, or the inappropriate use of assessment. This has a significant impact on children's progress, particularly those who are disadvantaged and those with SEND.

- Links with parents, other settings and professionals involved in supporting children's care and education do not identify or meet children's individual needs. Children fail to thrive.

- Leaders do not tackle instances of discrimination. Equality, Diversity and British Values are not actively promoted in practice.

- Safeguarding and welfare requirements are not met. Breaches have a significant impact on the safety and well-being of children.

OWN
Action Plan

HOW ARE YOU GOING TO IMPLEMENT THIS?

Intention

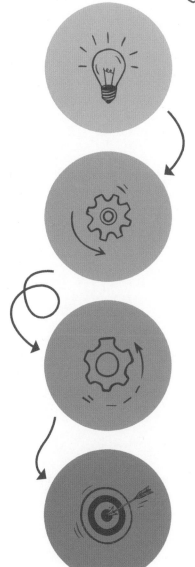

Impact ✔

MODULE TWO:
Lesson One

PROMPT
Call Sheet

Date of call:

Time of call:

Name of Ofsted inspector:

Name of additional inspector if attending:

Car details including registration:

Documents requested:

1.

2.

3.

4.

5.

6.

Time of estimated arrival:

Any other information needed?

Inform provider/owner:

MODULE TWO:
Lesson Two

CURRENT
List of Documents

Current staff list and their qualifications, including Paediatric First Aid certificates.

A register/list showing the date of birth of all children on roll and routine staff arrangements.

A list of the children who will be present at the setting during the inspection (if not shown on the register).

DBS records and any other documentation summarising the checks, vetting and employment arrangements of all staff working at the setting.

All logs that record accidents, exclusions, children taken off roll and incidents of poor behaviour.

All logs that record incidents of discrimination, including racist incidents.

A complaint log and/or evidence of any complaints and resolutions.

Fire-safety arrangements and other statutory policies relating to health and safety.

A list of any referrals made to the designated person for safeguarding, along with brief details of the resolutions.

Details of all the children who are an open case to social care/children's services and for who there is a multi-agency plan.

MODULE TWO:
Lesson Three

SETTING
Details

Manager's name:

Qualifications:

Deputy Manager's name:

SENCO:

Designated Safeguarding Lead:

Children on roll:

EAL Children:

SEN Children:

Qualifications of staff:

Level 6:

Number of agency staff:

Level 5:

Level 4:

Confirm all agency staff know safeguarding procedures: ✓

Level 3:

Level 2:

Confirm all staff's First Aid qualifications are up to date: ✓

Unqualified:

MODULE TWO:
Lesson Four

LINE
of Enquiry

Line of enquiry from last inspection:

What improvements have been made?

MODULE THREE: Lesson One

LEARNING
Walk

An excellent tool for settings

Any actions identified should feed into your self-evaluation.

Constantly think about what it's like for the child in your setting throughout this process.

Take time each week to ask a staff member to carry out the Learning Walk.

Use feedback to bring back to your staff meetings.

Use the RAG rating to help you decipher where you think you would be graded.

● = This is not happening

● = This happens but not consistently

● = This happens consistently

Name of person performing the Learning Walk:

Date:

Indoor Environment	Red	Amber	Green	Evidence, Comments and Actions
1. Is the room bright, well-organised and inviting to walk into? *Think about what is set at child height and what a child sees and feels.*	●	●	●	
2. Are these areas easily accessible for children and have an INTENT? *E.g. Role play, workshop/creative, sound experience, mark making, large and small construction, book, sand, water, malleable and tactile, small world*	●	●	●	
3. Is the room organised in ways that promote opportunities for children to talk and develop their communication skills? *E.g. Arrangement of home corner, location of book area*	●	●	●	
4. Are staff engaged in meaningful story time? Is there a purpose to the story? Are staff engaging in repetitive nursery rhymes?	●	●	●	
5. Are the resources and areas clean and fit for purpose? *E.g. Are resources to a good standard of repair?*	●	●	●	
6. Are resources age/stage appropriate?	●	●	●	
7. Does each activity have an INTENT?	●	●	●	
8. Are there a wide range of resources including natural, sensory and messy play?	●	●	●	
9. Are real life resources (recycled and reclaimed) used wherever possible? Do staff know the intent of why these are being used?	●	●	●	
10. Do the resources reflect all families and their cultural backgrounds? Are home language resources made visible within the environment?	●	●	●	

Indoor Environment	Red	Amber	Green	Evidence, Comments and Actions
11. Do displays include printed and handwritten titles, captions, photographs, children's own work and the child's voice? Do they celebrate children's achievements? Are they at child height?	●	●	●	
12. Are there interactive displays/areas which promote further exploration and promote critical thinking skills and language development?	●	●	●	
13. Can children display their own work as appropriate? *E.g. Low level boards, washing lines, low level shelving, opportunities for children to photograph their own work and use I.T. as a stimulus for reflection if needed*	●	●	●	
14. Can children access resources independently? Can they transport equipment to combine with other resources to further their learning?	●	●	●	
15. Does the room have areas for children to chill and have some downtime?	●	●	●	
16. Is purposeful play being monitored?	●	●	●	
17. Are there quiet areas for children to engage in conversation?	●	●	●	
18. Are visual resources available to promote talk about emotions and feelings?	●	●	●	
19. Have resources been identified to meet the specific needs of vulnerable groups? *E.g. EYPP, SEND premium, high needs, two year funding*	●	●	●	
20. Are there any 'invisible' children? *E.g. Are there any children who staff do not interact with and end up wandering around the setting without any engagement?*	●	●	●	
21. Are children with limited experiences being offered experiences which will promote and extend their learning?	●	●	●	
22. Is there an intention to the activities for the day?	●	●	●	
23. Can the key person recognise their key child's next steps and talk about how they are going to implement this?	●	●	●	

Indoor Environment	Red	Amber	Green	Evidence, Comments and Actions
24. Is the parents notice board easily accessible and complete with up-to-date information?	●	●	●	
25. Do children have the opportunity to access the outdoor area for extended periods of time each day in all weathers?	●	●	●	
26. Does the outdoor area compliment, rather than duplicate, indoor experiences?	●	●	●	
27. Is the area well-organised and inviting? Does it challenge and extend children's learning?	●	●	●	
28. Are there opportunities for children to become involved in physical play?	●	●	●	
29. Are children able to risk assess the setting themselves? Do they recognise how to keep themselves safe?	●	●	●	
30. Do children have the opportunity to explore natural materials and objects with a variety of different textures? *E.g. Mud kitchen, sand and water play (not necessarily in a tray), writing with sticks, making potions, open-ended play resources*	●	●	●	
31. Do children have the opportunity to investigate the natural environment? *E.g. Growing and planting, investigating minibeasts, seasonal changes, the environment*	●	●	●	
32. Are there opportunities for children to work on a large scale and develop their imaginations *E.g. Den building*	●	●	●	
33. Can children access and return resources independently?	●	●	●	
34. Are there relevant signs around the environment displaying meaningful print using natural resources?	●	●	●	

Indoor Environment	Red	Amber	Green	Evidence, Comments and Actions
35. Is there equipment of a variety of sizes to promote physical skills like throwing, catching etc?	●	●	●	
36. Is there a variety of good quality equipment to promote mark making on both a large and small scale?	●	●	●	
37. Have resources been identified and bought to meet the specific needs of vulnerable children? *E.g. EYPP, SEND premium, high needs, two year funding.*	●	●	●	
38. Are children with limited experiences being offered experiences which will promote and extend their learning?	●	●	●	
39. Does outdoor planning offer breadth and depth across all 7 areas of learning?	●	●	●	
40. How do you monitor areas to ensure purposeful play? Can staff identify when resources need to be added or taken away to stimulate purposeful play?	●	●	●	
41. Are staff able to demonstrate good knowledge on the Learning Walk and talk through confidently?	●	●	●	

Action Number	What is your INTENT to improve?	How are you going to IMPLEMENT this?	How will you measure the IMPACT?

MODULE FOUR:
Lesson One

QUALITY
of Education

Looking at the grade descriptors at the beginning of the course,
where do you feel you are sitting on the grading?

It is always good to evaluate each room, as well as the whole setting.

Grade:

Think about how you are going to improve on this?
What is your intention to help you improve?

How are you going to implement this ?

What will the IMPACT be?

MODULE FOUR:
Lesson Two

WRITE YOUR own Curriculum

WRITE YOUR
own Curriculum

Babies - Write statements about what you feel this
age group needs to learn before they move to Toddlers.

WRITE YOUR
own Curriculum

Toddlers - Write statements about what you feel this
age group needs to learn before they go to Older Toddlers.

WRITE YOUR
own Curriculum

Older Toddlers - Write statements about what you feel this age group needs before they go to Preschool.

WRITE YOUR
own Curriculum

Preschool - Write statements about what you feel this
age group needs to learn before they go to school.

MODULE FOUR:
Lesson Three

ACTIVITY
Evaluation

ACTIVITY
Evaluation

Date:

Room:

What is the INTENTION of the day?

How are we going to IMPLEMENT this?

What is the IMPACT?

Plan

ACTIVITY
Evaluation

Date:

Room:

What is the INTENTION of the day?

How are we going to IMPLEMENT this?

What is the IMPACT?

ACTIVITY
Evaluation

Date:

Room:

What is the INTENTION of the day?

How are we going to IMPLEMENT this?

What is the IMPACT?

Plan

ACTIVITY
Evaluation

Date:

Room:

What is the INTENTION of the day?

How are we going to IMPLEMENT this?

What is the IMPACT?

Plan

MODULE FOUR:
Lesson Four

OBSERVATION
Toolkit

PEER ON PEER
Observations

PEER ON PEER
Observations

Peer on Peer Observation Form.

Evaluation of Practitioner's Practice

Observer:

Practitioner observed:

Room:

Date:

Time:

Grading Criteria:

Outstanding	1	Consistently
Good	2	Mostly
Requires Improvement	3	Sometimes
Inadequate	4	Never

Add up the scores at the end of the observation to see where the practitioner's practice is.

	1	2	3	4
Does the practitioner engage in a conversation with children?	1	2	3	4
Does the practitioner watch and observe children before they engage in conversation?	1	2	3	4
Does the practitioner talk at an appropriate rate and make eye-contact?	1	2	3	4
Does the practitioner listen and respond to children?	1	2	3	4
Does the practitioner model language well?	1	2	3	4
Does the practitioner encourage children to express their thoughts and use new words?	1	2	3	4
Does the practitioner encourage independence and confidence in children?	1	2	3	4
Does the practitioner encourage children to speculate and test ideas through trial and error?	1	2	3	4
Does the practitioner enable children to explore and solve problems?	1	2	3	4

PEER ON PEER
Observations

Add up the scores at the end of the observation to see where the practitioner's practice is.

Does the practitioner behave as an excellent role model?	1	2	3	4
Does the practitioner support children to recognise and respond to their own physical needs?	1	2	3	4
Does the practitioner attend to children's personal needs?	1	2	3	4
Does the practitioner praise the child's achievements?	1	2	3	4
Does the practitioner provoke curiosity and critical thinking using open-ended questions?	1	2	3	4
Is the practitioner's body language warm and welcoming?	1	2	3	4
Are children engaged fully in their play?	1	2	3	4

Add up how many in each Grade Descriptor:

Outstanding	Mostly 1's
Good	Mostly 2's
Requires Improvement	Mostly 3's
Inadequate	Mostly 4's

Target to improve:

Date to achieve by:

LEADERS
AND
Managers Observations

LEADERS AND
Managers Observations

Evaluation of Practitioner's Practice

Observer:

Practitioner observed:

Room:

Date:

Time:

Grading Criteria:

Outstanding	**1**	Consistently
Good	**2**	Mostly
Requires Improvement	**3**	Sometimes
Inadequate	**4**	Never

Add up the scores at the end of the observation to see where the practitioner's practice is.

	1	2	3	4
Does the leader or manager ensure that all team are focused?	1	2	3	4
Does the leader or manager lead by example?	1	2	3	4
Does the leader or manager encourage children to take risks?	1	2	3	4
Does the leader or manager listen and respond to staff?	1	2	3	4
Does the leader or manager value contributions from their team?	1	2	3	4
Does the leader or manager see the bigger picture of the room and setup?	1	2	3	4
Does the leader or manager praise their team? Does the leader or manager take responsibility?	1	2	3	4
Is the leader or manager a good role model and demonstrates good practice?	1	2	3	4

LEADERS AND
Managers Observations

Add up the scores at the end of the observation to see where the practitioner's practice is.

	1	2	3	4
Does the leader or manager behave as an excellent role model?	1	2	3	4
Does the leader or manager remain positive and lead the team?	1	2	3	4
Does the leader or manager ensure the rooms activities have a purpose?	1	2	3	4
Does the leader or manager ensure all children are observed, assessed and planned for effectively?	1	2	3	4
Does the leader or manager have a vision and can they explain the purpose of the routine?	1	2	3	4
Does the leader introduce themselves to visitors who enter their room?	1	2	3	4
Are children and staff all fully engaged in their play?	1	2	3	4

Add up how many in each Grade Descriptor:

Outstanding	Mostly 1's
Good	Mostly 2's
Requires Improvement	Mostly 3's
Inadequate	Mostly 4's

Target to improve:

Date to achieve by:

BABIES
Observations

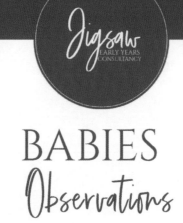

BABIES
Observations

Evaluation of Practitioner's Practice

Observer:

Practitioner observed:

Room:

Date:

Time:

Grading Criteria:

Outstanding	**1**	Consistently
Good	**2**	Mostly
Requires Improvement	**3**	Sometimes
Inadequate	**4**	Never

Add up the scores at the end of the observation to see where the practitioner's practice is.

	1	2	3	4
Does the practitioner maintain eye-contact when talking to parents?	1	2	3	4
Does the practitioner provide a detailed handover?	1	2	3	4
Does the practitioner say hello and welcome babies into the room?	1	2	3	4
Does the practitioner make eye-contact with babies when playing on the floor?	1	2	3	4
Does the practitioner model language well?	1	2	3	4
Does the practitioner repeat words for babies to mimic?	1	2	3	4
Does the practitioner encourage independence and confidence in children?	1	2	3	4
Does the practitioner meet babies personal needs, i.e. wiping noses and washing hands?	1	2	3	4
Does the practitioner provide different resources to promote new learning?	1	2	3	4

BABIES
Observations

Add up the scores at the end of the observation to see where the practitioner's practice is.

Does the practitioner encourage boundaries to keep babies safe?	1	2	3	4
Does the practitioner comfort babies when they become upset?	1	2	3	4
Does the practitioner interact with babies during nappy changing?	1	2	3	4
Does the practitioner praise the babies achievements?	1	2	3	4
Does the practitioner encourage fine and gross motor skills?	1	2	3	4
Is the practitioner's body language warm and welcoming?	1	2	3	4
Are babies engaged fully in their play?	1	2	3	4

Add up how many in each Grade Descriptor:

Outstanding	Mostly 1's
Good	Mostly 2's
Requires Improvement	Mostly 3's
Inadequate	Mostly 4's

Target to improve:

Date to achieve by:

STORIES AND
Rhymes Observations

STORIES AND
Rhymes Observations

Evaluation of Practitioner's Practice

Observer:

Practitioner observed:

Room:

Date:

Time:

Grading Criteria:

Outstanding	1	Consistently
Good	2	Mostly
Requires Improvement	3	Sometimes
Inadequate	4	Never

Add up the scores at the end of the observation to see where the practitioner's practice is.

	1	2	3	4
Does the practitioner maintain eye-contact when reading to children?	1	2	3	4
Does the practitioner introduce the story?	1	2	3	4
Does the practitioner sit at the children's level to make eye-contact when reading and singing?	1	2	3	4
Does the practitioner model language well?	1	2	3	4
Does the practitioner repeat words for children to copy?	1	2	3	4
Are all children engrossed and engaged in the story and rhyme time?	1	2	3	4
Does the practitioner use open-ended questions to create curiosity?	1	2	3	4
Does the practitioner encourage participation from the beginning of the story?	1	2	3	4
Does the practitioner maintain consistency when reading or singing?	1	2	3	4

STORIES AND
Rhymes Observations

Add up the scores at the end of the observation to see where the practitioner's practice is.

Are children focused when the practitioner is reading or singing?	1	2	3	4
Does the practitioner change their voice and try to engage children fully?	1	2	3	4
Does the practitioner give children enough time to answer questions?	1	2	3	4
Does the practitioner encourage all children to be involved?	1	2	3	4
Is the practitioner's body language warm and welcoming?	1	2	3	4

Add up how many in each Grade Descriptor:

Outstanding	Mostly 1's
Good	Mostly 2's
Requires Improvement	Mostly 3's
Inadequate	Mostly 4's

Target to improve:

Date to achieve by:

A FEW
Tips

- Keep the observations short – they shouldn't need to last longer than 10/15 minutes.

- Get staff to give a reason for the judgements they've made in the feedback session.

- Always give feedback in a private place.

- Try an 'observation week' instead of a specific time slot. That way practitioners don't necessarily know when they're going to be observed and won't feel they have to 'perform'.

- Make sure staff are honest but sensitive. No one should be made to feel like they are doing a bad job.

- Be a part of the feedback sessions if you think it will help staff to feel more comfortable.

- Always allow practitioners time to respond to feedback. Perhaps there's a reason for certain practice that the other staff member wasn't aware of.

- Be careful who you choose to pair up.

- Explain how peer observations help with their Early Years development and the children's outcomes.

- Explain the impact this can have on Early Years practice.

MODULE FOUR:
Lesson Five

Plan

MODULE FOUR:
Lesson Six

PROGRESS
Check at 2

PROGRESS
Check at 2

Early Years Foundation Stage (EYFS) two year old progress check:

Child's name:

Child's age/Date of birth: Date: Key person:

Child's learning:

Three Prime Areas:

Personal, Social and Emotional Development	Communication and Language	Physical Development

PROGRESS
Check at 2

Early Years Foundation Stage (EYFS) two year old progress check:

Child's name:

Child's age/Date of birth: Date: Key person:

Parent's comments:

Next steps:

What activities and resources will support next steps?

How can parents support next steps at home?

Parents/Carers signature: Key person signature: Moderated by:

MODULE FOUR:
Lesson Seven

VULNERABLE
Children

VULNERABLE
Children

Date:

Child's initials:

What is their need?

What are we doing to support the child?

How can we support the child further?

Do we need additional support?

Yes

No

If yes, what additional support do we need?

Once contact has been made, log the response:

MODULE FOUR:
Lesson Eight

JOINT
Observations

JOINT
Observation Form

Room:

Date:

Date:

Child's initials:

Practitioner being observed:

Activity being observed:

Inside/Outside	Number of children	Focused activity/Freeflow	Snack/Lunchtime

JOINT
Observation Form

Joint Observation Feedback

Feedback notes from observers:

Feedback from practitioners:

Action agreed and training required if any:

Signature of observers:

Signature of practitioners

MODULE FIVE:
Lesson One

BEHAVIOUR
and Attitudes

Looking at the grade descriptors in the beginning of the course, where do you feel you are sitting on the grading?

It is always good to evaluate each room as well as the whole setting.

Grade:

Think about how you are going to improve on this?
What is your intention to help you improve?

How are you going to implement this?

What will the IMPACT be?

MODULE SIX:
Lesson One

PERSONAL
Development

Looking at the grade descriptors in the beginning of the course,
where do you feel you are sitting on the grading?

It is always good to evaluate each room as well as the whole setting.

Grade:

Think about how you are going to improve on this?
What is your intention to help you improve?

How are you going to implement this?

What will the IMPACT be?

MODULE SIX:
Lesson Two

BRITISH
Values

BRITISH
Values

Take every section of the British Values and ask each room how they can demonstrate fundamental British Values every day.

Give examples:

Democracy:

Rule of Law:

BRITISH
Values

Take every section of the British Values and ask each room how they can demonstrate fundamental British Values every day.

Give examples:

Individual Liberty:

Mutual Respect and Tolerance:

MODULE SEVEN:
Lesson One

LEADERSHIP
and Management

Looking at the grade descriptors in the beginning of the course, where do you feel you are sitting on the grading?

It is always good to evaluate each room as well as the whole setting.

Grade:

Think about how you are going to improve on this?
What is your intention to help you improve?

How are you going to implement this?

What will the IMPACT be?

MODULE SEVEN:
Lesson Two

LEADERSHIP AND MANAGEMENT
Interview Questions

Leadership questions:	Name:	Date:

	Further questions:	● ● ●	Comments:

Admin

DBS records	Are all up to date?	● ● ●	
First Aid Certificates	Are all up to date?	● ● ●	
Registers	Are all up to date?	● ● ●	
Accident forms	Are all up to date?	● ● ●	
Incident forms	Are all up to date?	● ● ●	
Policies	Are all up to date?	● ● ●	
Records regarding safeguarding concerns and complaints	Are all up to date?	● ● ●	

Recruitment

1. Recruitment process	Discuss your recruitment process. Think about what questions you ask. *Who records this? Who interviews you? Are your questions effective? Do you allow applicants to do a stay and play session? If yes, why? If not, why not?*	● ● ●	
2. Reference checks	Who does this? What information do you ask for?	● ● ●	
3.	What would you do if a referee does not respond?	● ● ●	
4.	What would you do if you received worrying information about an applicant?	● ● ●	
5. Review	Review your most recent staffs' folder and compare it to one of your longest serving members of staff. What are the differences, if any?	● ● ●	
6.	Is there anything you do now that has developed /improved?	● ● ●	
7.	Is there anything you used to do that you might like to reintroduce?	● ● ●	

Induction

8.	When do you start inducting new staff? Discuss what this involves.	● ● ●	
9.	Who is responsible?	● ● ●	
10.	How do you know your induction procedures are effective?	● ● ●	
11.	When did you last review your induction procedures?	● ● ●	
12.	Are staff happy with the process?	● ● ●	
13.	Do they feel confident in their job role once their induction is complete? How do you know this?	● ● ●	
14.	How do you ensure that the information you have given them is secure in their minds?	● ● ●	

Supervision

15.	Discuss your supervision procedures. Are you confident in knowing them?	● ● ●	
16.	How frequent are they? Are they frequent enough?	● ● ●	
17.	Why are they done at these points? Are they adding impact?	● ● ●	
18.	Do you have specific templates for these sessions? If so, why?	● ● ●	
19.	Who is responsible for the supervision of staff? Is this effective?	● ● ●	
20.	Are all supervisions up to date? Can you prove it?	● ● ●	
21.	Do staff have action plans to work towards?	● ● ●	
22.	How often are these reviewed? Are they working?	● ● ●	
23.	It is worth considering that if an inspector identifies a weakness with a staff member which they or you are aware of then they will expect to see this documented and how the staff member is being supported to improve. Check out the documentation which includes targets and supervisions etc.	● ● ●	

Supervision

24.		What training and development opportunities do you provide your staff with? Inspectors will discuss this with your staff.	● ● ●	
25.		Don't forget YOU! Who carries out your supervision? Can you prove it?	● ● ●	
26.		What training and development opportunities do YOU have?	● ● ●	
27.		Peer observations - Do staff do this? If not, why not?	● ● ●	

Observation Assessment and Planning

28.		How do you as managers oversee what staff are planning with children?	● ● ●	
29.		What systems do you have in place to discuss the activities in the room and how they are supporting children's individual needs and stage of development?	● ● ●	
30.		Do you have any children on roll with additional needs? When was the last time this was reviewed?	● ● ●	
31.		Who is the SENCO and how do you work with them to ensure all children are making excellent progress?	● ● ●	

Safeguarding

| 32. | | How do you ensure that ALL staff have a faultless knowledge of your procedures and practices? Inspectors WILL talk to staff about safeguarding and ask them what they would do in certain situations. Making a mistake with safeguarding is not an option. It will have an impact on your judgement if staff don't know what to do in order to keep children safe. | ● ● ● | |

Safeguarding

33.	How often do you discuss safeguarding with your staff? This should be ongoing.	● ● ●	
34.	Is this effective? How often do they have training?	● ● ●	
35.	Do you use external companies? *E.g. French teachers, music and movement providers etc., coming into the setting to work with the children? How do you know they are suitable?*	● ● ●	
36.	Who is the designated lead and when was the last time they were trained? Check it is every 2 years.	● ● ●	
37.	Have you had any safeguarding concerns since your last inspection? Be prepared to discuss these and the procedures you followed.	● ● ●	

Self - Evaluation

38.	Self-evaluation, action plans, continuous development whatever it is you call it, the inspector will want to discuss and see it.	● ● ●	
39.	How have you improved /developed since your last inspection?	● ● ●	
40.	What were your previous actions/ recommendations from Ofsted?	● ● ●	
41.	How have you worked towards these?	● ● ●	
42.	Where is your evidence? How do you include staff, parents and children in your self-evaluation? Where is your evidence?	● ● ●	
43.	Inspectors may ask staff about training they have attended and how this has helped them improve their practice and learning outcomes for children.	● ● ●	

44.	Is communication with parents effective? How do you engage all parents in their children's learning and share information about their development? Can you prove it?	● ● ●	
45.	How have you collaborated with parents during lockdown? What worked and what didn't?	● ● ●	
46.	Do you have parents' evenings /afternoons/1-1 times? Are these effective?	● ● ●	
47.	How do you engage those parents that are hard to reach? By admitting that you have parents that don't respond, you have just written your recommendation...	● ● ●	
48.	Do you have any children on roll who are supported by other agencies or professionals? *E.g. speech and language, Portage, social worker? If you have, then chances are these children will have been tracked during the inspection.*	● ● ●	
49.	As managers, you will be expected to be able to discuss how you liaise with other professionals and the family to help provide a consistent approach to their care and learning. Make sure you have evidence to show the collaboration.	● ● ●	
50.	Do you have any children on roll who attend other settings? A common response is 'yes but they don't share the information with us'. Make sure you have evidence of what you have sent to them and print outs of emails with dates on with your attempts to make contact.	● ● ●	

WHAT ARE YOUR ACTIONS
from your Findings?

Make sure they are SMART.

MODULE SEVEN:
Lesson Three

SAFEGUARDING
Audit

SETTING
Details

Name of setting:

Address including postcode:

Name of registered person:

Name of manager:

Ofsted URN:

Name(s) of person(s) completing form:

Role(s) of person(s) completing form:

Date of last inspection:

Email address:

SAFEGUARDING
Audit

Date of audit:

We suggest you use the method of a RAG rating to grade
your setting to ensure you are prioritizing your actions.

RAG rating:

⚫ = Requires immediate action

⚫ = System in place, needs to be embedded within practice

⚫ = Robust system in place with no action required

Part 1: Safer Recruitment and safer working practices	RAG Rating	Yes *Record supporting evidence*	No *Record action required*
1. Has someone in your setting completed training in Safer Recruitment? • Settings must recruit staff and volunteers following Safer Recruitment procedures. • There is an expectation that at least one member of staff/committee that would sit on an interview panel, has attended the required Safer Recruitment training. • The Safer Recruitment training must be repeated every five years.	⚫⚫⚫	Name(s): Date(s):	
1.1 Do job descriptions and person specifications include safeguarding responsibilities? • Ensure that you have an up to date job description and person specification for the role(s) you wish to recruit. • These should specify the individual's responsibilities in regard to safeguarding.	⚫⚫⚫		
1.2 Is induction training available for all staff? Induction training must include: • Information about emergency evacuation procedures • Safeguarding • Child protection • Health and safety issues	⚫⚫⚫		

Part 1: Safer Recruitment and safer working practices	RAG Rating	Yes Record supporting evidence	No Record action required
1.2 And also: • Code of conduct/staff behaviour policy • Whistleblowing • Allegations	●●●		
1.3 Does your setting have a record and evidence of all recruitment checks? • Providers must record information about staff qualifications and the identity checks and vetting processes have been completed. This will include the Criminal Disclosure reference number, the date the disclosure was obtained, and details of who obtained it. • Two references for every successful candidate.	●●●		
1.4 Have all staff in the setting had an Enhanced DBS check with barred list checks? • Do all staff who have regular, unsupervised contact with children hold a satisfactory Enhanced DBS/CRB Disclosure with a Children's Barred List check?	●●●		
1.5 If you are a voluntary group, have all management committee members had Enhanced DBS checks?	●●●		
1.6 Have parents/carers who regularly support their children or volunteers who come into the setting had an Enhanced DBS check?	●●●		
1.7 Do you have up to date risk assessments on any staff where there has been information released on their DBS?	●●●		
1.8 Has the 'suitability' under the Childcare Act 2006 been recorded for each member of staff?	●●●		

Part 2: Temporary staff and students	RAG Rating	Yes *Record supporting evidence*	No *Record action required*
2.1 Are recruitment checks carried out on any temporary/supply staff and details recorded? Temporary/supply staff employed directly by the setting must have had recruitment checks and their details recorded.	● ● ●		
2.2 Does your setting have written confirmation from training providers that all students hold Enhanced DBS check with Children's Barred List checks included? It is the responsibility of the training provider to ensure that all students visiting settings hold a satisfactory Enhanced DBS Disclosure, including Children's Barred List in 'regulated' activities. Secondary school/6th form students on work experience do not need to be DBS checked. In these cases the school placing the student should ensure that the young person is suitable for the placement.	● ● ●		

Part 3: Visitors and contracted staff	RAG Rating	Yes *Record supporting evidence*	No *Record action required*
3.1 Does your setting have a signing-in system for visitors? Any visitor entering the setting must be asked to prove their identity and to sign in and out however familiar they may be with the children or staff. Visitors must not be left unsupervised with children in the setting. Reasonable steps must be taken to prevent access to buildings and outdoor play areas by unauthorised persons.	● ● ●		
3.2 Does your setting have written confirmation of recruitment and DBS checks on professionals who regularly visit the setting? This could include: ● Early Years Advisory Teachers and Officers ● Health Visitors ● Assessors	● ● ●		

Part 4: Designated Person	RAG Rating	Yes *Record supporting evidence*	No *Record action required*
4.1 Does your setting have a designated lead person for safeguarding who has been trained in the last 2 years? • Each setting must have a designated lead person for safeguarding, who is named, appropriately trained and known to all staff and parents. • They must provide support, advice and guidance to any other staff on an ongoing basis and on any specific safeguarding issue as required. • It is necessary to have at least two people in this role, to cover staff absence, or where the designated person does not work every day. • This person cannot be a member of the committee.	● ● ●	Name(s): Date(s):	
4.2 Do you have contingency plans in place to ensure there is always a named Safeguarding Lead on duty to cover arrangements such as annual leave or sickness?	● ● ●	Name(s): Date(s):	

Part 5: Staff training and supervision	RAG Rating	Yes *Record supporting evidence*	No *Record action required*
5.1 Have all other staff attended safeguarding to the correct level of training required by your local authority?	● ● ●		
5.2 Are all staff given the opportunity to receive regular updates on safeguarding and child protection at least annually?	● ● ●		
5.3 Is there at least one person who holds a current Paediatric First Aid certificate on the premises at all times, when children are present and who accompanies children on outings?	● ● ●		
5.4 Have ALL staff completed PREVENT training?	● ● ●		
5.5 Do all staff have regular supervision meetings? The EYFS requires that all staff must have regular individual supervision meetings with their manager to discuss any issues, particularly concerning children's development or well-being. Identify solutions to address issues as they arise including 'safeguarding' as a routine item for discussion. Receive coaching to improve their personal effectiveness.	● ● ●		
5.6 Have all staff completed Child Sexual Exploitation Training?	● ● ●		

Part 6: Policies and procedures	RAG Rating	Yes *Record supporting evidence*	No *Record action required*
6.1 Do you have a child protection/safeguarding policy in place which is in line with the local safeguarding partners policy?	● ● ●		
6.2 Is the telephone number for the Multi-Agency Safeguarding Hub (MASH) readily available in the setting?	● ● ●		
6.3 Do your policies and procedures refer to all aspects of personal care? This will include: • Sleep • Nappy changing • Managing children who are sick and or infectious • Managing children with allergies • Food and drink	● ● ●		
6.4 Does your setting have a whistle-blowing policy/procedure? If staff or volunteers have genuine concerns about malpractice, unsafe or unlawful activities in the setting, they can report this by following the correct procedures and their employment rights are protected.	● ● ●		
6.5 Does your setting have a policy on the use of mobile phones and cameras? • You must ensure that staff do not carry or use personal mobile phones and cameras whilst working in the setting. • The setting should have its own mobile phone or landline and use only the setting's camera. • Visitors must not use mobile phones in the setting. • Visitors' use of cameras to be in line with settings policy. • Staff, visitors, and parents must abide by the Acceptable User Policy.	● ● ●		
6.6 Does your setting have an administration of medication policy/procedure? Providers must have and implement a policy and procedures, for administering medicines. It must include systems for obtaining information about a child's needs for medicines, and for keeping this information up-to-date. • Medicines must not usually be administered unless they have been prescribed for a child by a doctor, dentist, nurse, or pharmacist (medicines containing aspirin should only be given if prescribed by a doctor).	● ● ●		

Part 6: Policies and procedures	RAG Rating	Yes *Record supporting evidence*	No *Record action required*
• Providers must only administer medicines to a child where written permission for that particular medicine has been obtained from the child's parents and/or carer. • Training must be provided for staff where the administration of medicine requires medical or technical knowledge. • Providers must keep a written record each time a medicine is administered to a child, and inform the child's parents and/or carers on the same day, or as soon as reasonably practicable.	● ● ●		
6.7 Does your setting have a procedure to be followed in the event of a parent failing to collect a child at the appointed time?	● ● ●		
6.8 Does your setting have a procedure to be followed in the event of a child going missing at, or away from the setting?	● ● ●		
6.9 Does your setting have an accident or injury procedure?	● ● ●		
6.10 Are Risk Assessments in place? Providers must ensure that they take all reasonable steps to ensure staff and children in their care are not exposed to risks and must be able to demonstrate how they are managing risks (EYES 3.64).	● ● ●		
6.11 Does your setting have an emergency evacuation procedure? Providers must have an emergency evacuation procedure.	● ● ●		
6.12 Does your setting have a named practitioner responsible for promoting positive behaviour?	● ● ●		

Part 7: Information for parents/carers	RAG Rating	Yes *Record supporting evidence*	No *Record action required*
7.1 Does the information you provide for new parents/carers explain who owns or runs the setting? You can demonstrate this through your leaflet, prospectus or website.	● ● ●		
7.2 Does your information tell parents/carers how to make a complaint about the setting, or who to contact if they have a concern about it?	● ● ●		
7.3 Does your information tell parents/carers about your safeguarding responsibilities? It is important to make them aware that you have a duty to report safeguarding concerns about children in the setting.	● ● ●		
7.4 Does your information tell parents/carers how to report a safeguarding concern about a child?	● ● ●		

AFTER
the Audit

Now you have completed the Audit

What is your INTENT?

What do you need to IMPLEMENT?

How will you measure the IMPACT?

MODULE SEVEN:
Lesson Four

POLICIES
AND
Procedures

LIST OF
Policies and Procedures

Use this space to list your policies and procedures
and record the last time they were updated.

MODULE SEVEN:
Lesson Five

SAFER
RECRUITMENT
Checklist

STEPS TO
Safer Recruitment

Steps to safer recruitment	In place and consistent	Needs Improving	Not in place	Prioritised actions for quality improvement: *What needs to happen?*
Planning and advertising:				
Clear job description in place This states: • The main duties of the post. • The extent of contact/responsibility for children and young people. • The individual's responsibility for promoting and safeguarding the welfare of the children/young people.				
Personal specification in place This includes: • The essential and desirable qualifications and experience. • Other requirements needed to perform the role in relation to working with children and young people. • The competencies and qualities that the successful candidate should be able to demonstrate.				
Post advertised as widely as possible.				
Advert states: • Commitment to safeguarding children. • The need for the successful applicant to undertake an enhanced criminal record check. • That proof of identity will be required.				
Final date stated for applications and interview date if known.				
Advert states that referees will be contacted prior to interview.				

Steps to safer recruitment	In place and consistent	Needs Improving	Not in place	Prioritised actions for quality improvement: *What needs to happen?*
Planning and advertising:				

Standard application form used obtain a common set of core data.
 	
It seeks to obtain:
 	
• Identifying details of the applicant including current and former names, current address and National Insurance Number.
 	
• N.B. To comply with the Equality Act 2010, recruiting bodies may wish to adopt a practice that the date of birth should not be included on the main application form, but added to a diversity monitoring form, which can be retained by HR/Personnel and not made available to those involved in the short-listing process.
 	
• A statement of any academic and/or vocational qualifications with details of awarding body and date of award.
 	
• A full history in chronological order since leaving secondary education, including periods of any post-secondary education/training and part-time and voluntary work as well as full time employment, with start dates, explanations for periods not in employment or education/training and reasons for leaving employment.
 	
• Details of referees. One referee should be the applicant's current or most recent employer/line manager, not a colleague. Normally two referees are needed.
 	
  • Where an applicant is not currently working with children, but has done so in the past, it is important that a reference is also obtained from the employer by whom the person was most recently employed in work with children in addition to the current or most recent employer.
 	
  • References are not accepted from relatives or friends.				

Steps to safer recruitment	In place and consistent	Needs Improving	Not in place	Prioritised actions for quality improvement: *What needs to happen?*
Planning and advertising:				
• A statement of the skills and abilities, and competencies/experience that the applicant believes are relevant to his/her suitability for the post and how s/he meets the person specification. • There is an explanation that the post is exempt from the Rehabilitation of Offenders Act 1974. • Information is requested about any previous, including spent, convictions, cautions, reprimands or warnings.				
Information pack sent to applicants. The pack includes a copy of: • The application form, and explanatory notes about completing the form. • The job description and person specification. • Relevant information about the organisation and the recruitment process. • The setting's Safeguarding Policy. • A statement of the terms and conditions relating to the post.				
Permission sought to obtain references prior to interview.				
Shortlisting:				
Shortlisting is undertaken by a minimum of two people.				
At least one member of the panel has undertaken Safe Recruitment and selection training.				
The same selection panel both short list and interview the candidate.				

Steps to safer recruitment	In place and consistent	Needs Improving	Not in place	Prioritised actions for quality improvement: *What needs to happen?*
Shortlisting:				
Applications are reviewed against essential and desirable criteria.				
Information is checked for consistency and discrepancies.				
Gaps in employment/training or a history of repeated changes of employment are identified and noted so that they are taken up as part of the consideration of whether to short list the applicant, or to ask the applicant for further explanation at interview.				
Incomplete applications are not accepted.				
Referees contacted for all shortlisted candidates before interview.				
Interview:				
Consideration given to what assessment methods as well as interviews may be used.				
Interview panel established of a minimum of two people.				
All first interviews are face to face meetings or via online platform during pandemic.				
Candidates asked at interview about: • Any anomalies, discrepancies identified on their application form. • Any gaps in their employment history. • Criminal convictions and/or concerns /allegations/investigations. • Their motivation for working with children. • Their understanding of the roles safeguarding responsibilities. • Any issues arising from their references.				

Steps to safer recruitment	In place and consistent	Needs Improving	Not in place	Prioritised actions for quality improvement: *What needs to happen?*
Interview:				
List of questions prepared that assess each candidate against the job description and person specification.				
Clear notes are recorded of the candidates' responses at interview and stored securely.				
The interview stresses that the identity of the successful candidate will be checked thoroughly and, that where a Disclosure and Barring Service check is appropriate, prior to appointment there will be a requirement to complete an application for a Disclosure and Barring Service disclosure.				
All candidates bring with them documentary evidence of their right to work in the UK and their identity. Evidence should be as prescribed by UK Visas and Immigration and the Disclosure and Barring Service, and can include a current driving licence or passport including a photograph, or a full birth certificate, and a document such as a utility bill or financial statement that shows the candidate's current name and address. Please note that these latter two are time-limited and must be no more than 3 months old. Where appropriate, change of name documentation and some form of photographic ID is seen.				
Candidates bring documents confirming any educational and professional qualification(s). If this is not possible, written confirmation is obtained from the awarding body.				
A copy of the documents used to verify the successful candidate's identity and qualifications are kept for the personnel file.				

Steps to safer recruitment	In place and consistent	Needs Improving	Not in place	Prioritised actions for quality improvement: *What needs to happen?*
Offer of employment:				
Candidates are informed that any offers of employment are conditional and dependant on checks.				
References:				
Professional references for the preferred candidate taken up if not already done prior to interview. Once received any concerns resolved satisfactorily before the person's appointment is confirmed.				
A copy of the job description and person specification is included with all reference requests.				
References include one from the candidate's current employer from their line manager or HR department.				
References obtained from a previous employer involving childcare if the candidate is not currently working in childcare to confirm details of their employment and reason(s) for leaving.				
Character references (from friends or relatives) are not accepted.				
'Open-ended'/'To whom it may concern' references are not accepted.				
References are sought on all short listed candidates, including internal ones.				
Checks are made that any written references are from the named referee.				
Reference proforma in place to obtain objective verifiable information.				

Steps to safer recruitment	In place and consistent	Needs Improving	Not in place	Prioritised actions for quality improvement: *What needs to happen?*
References:				
Requests for references ask: • The referee's relationship with the candidate. *E.g. Did they have a working relationship and how long has the referee known the candidate.* • How they have demonstrated that they meet the person specification. • Whether the referee is satisfied that the person has the ability and is suitable to undertake the job. • Whether the applicant has been the subject of any disciplinary sanctions and whether the application has had any allegations made against them or concerns raised, which relate either to the safety and welfare of, or the applicants behaviour towards, children and young people. Details about the outcome of any such concern is sought. • Whether the referee is satisfied that the candidate is suitable to work with children/young people/adults at risk. If not, for details of the referee's concerns and the reason why the person might be unsuitable. • Confirmation of details of the applicant's current post, salary and sickness record. • Specific verifiable comments about the applicant's performance history and conduct. • Requests remind the referee that they have a responsibility to ensure that the reference is accurate and that relevant factual content of the reference may be discussed with the applicant.				
On receipt of references: • They are checked to ensure all questions have been answered satisfactorily.				

Steps to safer recruitment	In place and consistent	Needs Improving	Not in place	Prioritised actions for quality improvement: *What needs to happen?*
References:				
• Prior to the confirmation of an appointment, referees are telephoned to confirm their views on the candidate and to ensure information provided by the candidate is accurate.				
• Any information about past disciplinary action or allegations is considered in the circumstances of the individual case. Cases in which an issue was satisfactorily resolved some time ago or an allegation determined to be unfounded or did not require formal disciplinary sanctions, and in which no further issues have been raised, are less likely to cause concern than more serious or recent concerns, or issues that were not resolved satisfactorily. A history of repeated concerns or allegations over time should give cause for concern.				
Pre-employment checks:				
An offer of appointment to the successful candidate is conditional upon: • Receipt of at least two satisfactory written references. Confirmation via telephone is needed for all. • Verification of the candidate's identity. • A satisfactory Disclosure and Barring Service Disclosure at the appropriate level (unless the Disclosure and Barring Service Update Service applies). • Evidence of permission to work for those who are not nationals of a European Economic Area (EEA) country. • Verification of the candidate's medical fitness. • Verification of qualifications. • Verification of successful completion of statutory induction/probationary period where appropriate.				

Steps to safer recruitment	In place and consistent	Needs Improving	Not in place	Prioritised actions for quality improvement: *What needs to happen?*
Pre-employment checks:				
All checks are: • Confirmed in writing. • Documented and retained on the personnel file (subject to restrictions on the retention of information imposed by Disclosure and Barring Service regulations). • Followed up where they are unsatisfactory or where there are discrepancies in the information provided. • Recorded on the DBS log detailing the date when the disclosure was obtained, by whom, level of disclosure and unique reference number.				
Risk assessment procedures in place to determine whether or not the individual is suitable to undertake the role where a DBS disclosure trace is returned giving consideration to: • The nature of the appointment. • The nature of the offence. • The age at which the offence took place. • The frequency of the offence. Where: • The candidate is found to be on the Barred Lists, or the Disclosure and Barring Service Disclosure shows they have been disqualified from working with children by a Court. • The applicant has provided false information in, or in support of, their application. • There are serious concerns about an applicant's suitability to work with children.				

Steps to safer recruitment	In place and consistent	Needs Improving	Not in place	Prioritised actions for quality improvement: *What needs to happen?*
Pre-employment checks:				
• These facts are reported to the police and/or Disclosure and Barring Service (if they are not already aware). Anyone who is barred from work with children is committing an offence if they apply for, offer to do, accept or do any work which constitutes regulated activity. It is also an offence for an employer knowingly to offer work in a regulated position, or to procure work in a regulated position for an individual who is disqualified from working with children, or fail to remove such an individual from such work.				
Starting employment:				
In relation to each member of staff appointed a record is kept to show: • Written references obtained and confirmed by telephone. • Gaps in employment history checked. • A satisfactory Disclosure and Barring Service /Enhanced Disclosure and Barring Service certificate obtained, with unique reference number and date. • Reasons/decision to appoint despite criminal convictions (i.e. a Risk Assessment). • Evidence of proof of identity (this will have been provided for the Disclosure and Barring Service check). • Evidence of qualifications. • Details of registration with appropriate professional body. • Confirmation of right to work in UK. • Record of interview questions and answers. Records are signed and dated by appointing manager/chair of the interview panel.				

Steps to safer recruitment	In place and consistent	Needs Improving	Not in place	Prioritised actions for quality improvement: *What needs to happen?*
Starting employment:				
Thorough induction procedures in place which include: • Training and information about the organisation's safeguarding and child protection policies and procedures. This training is at a level appropriate to the member of staff role and responsibilities with regard to children. • Supporting individuals in a way that is appropriate for their role. • Confirming the conduct expected of staff. • Providing opportunities for a new member of staff or volunteer to discuss any issues or concerns about their role or responsibilities. • Enabling the line manager or mentor to recognise any concerns or issues about the person's ability or suitability at the outset and address them immediately. The person receives written statements of: • Policies and procedures in relation to safeguarding. • The identity and responsibilities of staff with designated safeguarding responsibilities. • Safe practice and the standards of conduct and behaviour expected. • Other relevant personnel procedures. *E.g. Whistle blowing, disciplinary procedures.*				
Supervision and staff review and development:				
Regular and ongoing staff reviews are embedded in practice. These reviews: • Ensure staff are up to date with current safe practices.				

Steps to safer recruitment	In place and consistent	Needs Improving	Not in place	Prioritised actions for quality improvement: *What needs to happen?*
Supervision and staff review and development:				
• Identify and support areas for development. • Openly address any concerns about behaviour and attitudes. • Provide an opportunity to raise concerns about key children. • Support staff well-being. • Put in place action plan and arrangements for review.				

Supporting information and further guidance:

Equality Act 2010

Keeping children safe in education (2021)

Disclosure and Barring Service website

Statutory guidance: Regulated Activity (children) - supervision of activity with children which is regulated activity when unsupervised

Care Quality Commission – Disclosure and Barring Service Checks

Guidance for safer working practice for those working with children and young people in education settings

Statutory Guidance: Disqualification under the Childcare Act 2006

MODULE SEVEN:
Lesson Six

PARTNERSHIPS

QUESTIONS
for Staff

Write down the questions you feel you would
want to be asked in your questionnaire.

EXAMPLE OF
Staff Questionnaire

Dear staff member,

As part of our self-evaluation, we are constantly striving to improve on our practice and would appreciate your willingness to share your views on this. All answers will be treated anonymously. Please place a cross in the box to indicate your answer.

We will collate the information and send out a report to you summarising our findings and any actions that we are going to take as a result.

Scale: Strongly Agree = 4   Agree = 3   Disagree = 2   Strongly Disagree = 1

Statement	4	3	2	1
I find it rewarding to be a member of the team at this setting				
I feel I am listened to regarding my own well-being				
I am encouraged to be part of the team and share best practice with my colleagues within my setting				
I am given the chance to share best practice with colleagues from other settings				
I have a clear understanding of the vision of the setting				
I am supported to engage in professional learning				
Staff members treat each other with respect				
Staff members treat children with respect				
Children are encouraged to treat each other with respect				
Parents and staff treat each other with respect				
Staff members are aware on how to manage children's behaviour				
Staff members at all levels communicate effectively with each other				
Staff members effectively engage all parents in their child's learning				
The setting is well-led and managed				
All children are engaged in their learning				
Children are provided with experiences which meet their learning and development needs				
Children are involved in the planning of their learning process				
I receive support with my development				
I am listened to and I want to make changes to the way my room is run				
I am actively involved in the setting's self-evaluation				
I understand the settings procedure relating to safeguarding and child protection				

Any other comments:

Date:

WORKING
in Partnerships

Outside Agencies Questionnaires

Building on from working in partnership with parents and staff and using the questionnaires to summarise your findings, consider doing the same for working in partnership with other settings. This also can be done anonymously, either by (i) sending out forms to the settings you work with or by (ii) creating a Google form where you can send the link and the responses will come through.

Examples of Partnership Questions

1. How long have you been working in partnership with the setting?

2. Do we work in partnership on a regular basis?

3. Do you feel you are being listened to?

4. Do you know our safeguarding policy and procedure?

5. How does your setting provide relevant information about the needs of the children?

6. Does our setting value the contribution made by your organisation?

7. Does the setting share best practices and networking with others?

8. How does the setting work overall in partnership with yourselves?

QUESTIONS
for Others

Write down the questions you feel you need to ask
others who work with you. E.g. Outside agencies.

MODULE SEVEN:
Lesson Seven

COMPLAINTS

COMPLAINTS

Date of complaint:

Source of complaint - tick appropriate box:

Parent (in writing, including email):

Parent (in person):

Parent (phone call):

Staff member:

Anonymous:

Ofsted (Complaint number if known):

Other please state:

Nature of complaint - Please tick the requirements that the complaint relates to:

Early Years complaint:

Childcare Register complaint:

COMPLAINTS

Tick the area which the complaint resides under:

Leadership and management	☐	Learning and development	☐
Safeguarding	☐	Suitable people	☐
Smoking	☐	Medication and other substances	☐
Food and drink	☐	Outings	☐
Accident and injuries	☐	SEN	☐
Behaviour management	☐	Information and records	☐
Complaints	☐		☐

Details of complaint:

COMPLAINTS

How was it dealt with? *Please tick as appropriate.*

Internal investigation

Investigation by Ofsted

Investigation by other agencies

Please give details of any internal investigation or attach an outcome letter from Ofsted:

Actions and outcomes - *please tick as appropriate.*

Internal actions

Actions agreed with Ofsted

Changes to conditions of registration

Other action taken by Ofsted

No action

Actions imposed or agreed with other agencies

COMPLAINTS

Please give details:

Has a copy of this record been shared with parents?

Yes: No:

Name of recorder:

Position:

Outcome notified to parent?

Yes: No:

Date: Date completed:

Signature:

Confirm this is placed in complaints file:

Yes: No:

MODULE SEVEN:
Lesson Eight

TRAINING

TRAINING
Attended

Name of staff member:	Training attended:	Date:

TRAINING
Evaluation Sheet

Name of staff member:

Name of course:

What is the INTENT?

How are you going to implement the INTENT?

What was the IMPACT of the training?

MODULE SEVEN:
Lesson Nine

SUPERVISION
Tracker

Name of staff member	1	2	3	4	5	6	7	8	9	10	11	12	13	14	15

Name of staff member	16	17	18	19	20	21	22	23	24	25	26	27	28	29	30	31

MODULE SEVEN:
Lesson Ten

WELL-BEING
Questionnaire

The questions below ask you how you feel regarding your well-being at work. You have the option of 5 responses ranging from 1 (Never), through to 5 (All the time). The questionnaire is a good way for everyone to review how you and your colleagues are feeling within the setting.

The responses can be used to measure the team's current feelings and enable managers to plan any areas that may need further attention. If you have any issues to raise in regards to your workload or well-being, talk to your line manager, owner or director who will be able to help.

Name:

Role:

Date:

1. I know what is expected of me at work.

1	2	3	4	5

Further comments:

2. People know my job role and responsibilities.

1	2	3	4	5

Further comments:

3. I feel like someone at work cares about me as a person.

1   2   3   4   5

Further comments:

4. I have good relationships with my staff.

1   2   3   4   5

Further comments:

5. I have good relationships with both children and parents.

1   2   3   4   5

Further comments:

6. There is someone at work who encourages my personal development.

1   2   3   4   5

Further comments:

7. I have opportunities to be listened to.

1   2   3   4   5

Further comments:

8. I generally enjoy my work.

1   2   3   4   5

Further comments:

9. I feel like I do my job well.

1   2   3   4   5

Further comments:

10. I feel like I can manage my workload.

1   2   3   4   5

Further comments:

11. I know who I can talk to if I feel stressed or anxious.

1   2   3   4   5

Further comments:

12. I feel like I am treated fairly at work.

1   2   3   4   5

Further comments:

13. I understand what my setting is trying to achieve for the children in our care.

1   2   3   4   5

Further comments:

14. I feel like I have responsibility in helping my setting achieve its aim.

1   2   3   4   5

Further comments:

15. I have the chance to use my strengths and abilities at work.

| 1 | 2 | 3 | 4 | 5 |

Further comments:

16. I enjoy coming to work.

| 1 | 2 | 3 | 4 | 5 |

Further comments:

WELL-BEING
Follow-up

If a follow-up meeting is required after comments made on the Well-Being Questionnaire, the line manager/owner/director can use this page to record any conversations, actions or targets with a review date to discuss the impact.

Printed in Poland
by Amazon Fulfillment
Poland Sp. z o.o., Wrocław